TINA MOSELY

God, Thank You for Building Character in Me

First edition

Editing & Interior by Paula McDade

Published by Stellar Creative LLC

Contents

Foreword

This book is about being empowered. This devotional is about inspiring you to reflect back on your own life experiences and then be willing to make adjustments in your own life and trust yourself to allow yourself the opportunity to grow in your daily life journey.

This book is about you critically taking the time to stop and evaluate your own personal journey and finding a new beginning where you can take ownership of the old and learn to grow in the "new" process and be developed.

This book is for every man and woman boy and girl this book will reach every age. This book will speak to you and meet you where you are at This book will cause you to self-exam yourself and challenge you to push yourself to the limit and become a person of excellence.

This book will cause you to see that you are not alone. That you are not the only one who is or has gone through the storms, trials, battles, and the conditions of life.

This book will teach you to hold yourself accountable and relate the devotional to the scripture for the day.

Throughout this devotional you will have taken a personal perspective and inventory of anything that you considered to be a crushing blow at one point or another in your life, this book also serves as a tool to break any self-defeating thoughts and behaviors and the goal is to replace them with the word of God, His truth, love, and guidance for your life.

Hopefully, one of the things that you will also take away from this book is learning how to separate yourself from the busyness of life's events and begin to realize that more time has to be spent on developing, growing, and maturing in the word of God so that you can have a life that is full of joy, peace, laughter, and fellowship.

In final closing thoughts, I just want to take a few moments to thank the Lord and Savior Jesus Christ for anointing my hands, my mind, my soul, my body to complete this book. For it is not in my strength but the strength of the Lord that He anointed my hands to do the work and pray for every person that would read this book that you will have such a new experience.

I pray for a new encounter and for some of you who will read this devotional this will be the beginning of a new relationship. It is my personal prayer, mission, and mandate that your life be forever changed and cultivated through new lenses to look at life from a kingdom perspective (outlook) now.

May this devotional meet each and every one of you at your appointed place and time in destiny to find your personal voice and give you a new confidence and strength that you did not have prior to reading this.

May this book bless you for the rest of your life and may you go and tell the good news to others!

Many abundant blessings unto you!

Oh Lord, How Great Is Thy Faithfulness!

DAY ONE

Lamentations 3:23 New Living Translation (NLT)

Great is his faithfulness; his mercies begin afresh each morning.

Oh, how precious and wonderful is this news! God is great and worthy to be praised! Beloved, God cares very very deeply for you. I want you to know that the Holy Spirit is concerned about your every thought, every worry, every stress, and every anxiety that you have.

I want to encourage you to begin to trust in the Lord with all of your heart… your complete heart. Trust me, give everything to him. He can handle it all! You don't have to hold onto anything.

Let me witness and speak to you that God has unfailing loving strong, confident, capable, efficient unchanging hands. He is powerful, mighty, confident, dependable, reliable, and always right on time! So, now that I have described how good God is I want to suggest that you try him for yourself.

Allow God to be your healer and wash your diseases- sickness, infection, complaints, condition, troubles, disabilities, virus, wounds, and all of your afflictions away today!

This very moment! Won't you let him have a chance? You have tried everything else. Just trust God and see that he is real. His mercies are new each morning. What's stopping you? Real Talk!

Your Valley Experience

DAY TWO

Psalm 23 Amplified Bible, Classic Edition (AMPC) **A Psalm of David.**
The Lord is my Shepherd [to feed, guide, and shield me], I shall not lack.

During this time allow the Holy Spirit to begin a work in you. You may feel like you just can't take it anymore. You may feel as if you are all alone, you don't have anyone to talk to, or as if you simply just can't take it anymore. Trust me dear one, you are okay.

You are exactly where you are supposed to be, and you are learning the stages of process and development. In the Twenty Third Psalm we are reminded that the Lord is our Shepherd, he feeds, guides, and protects us on a daily basis. Go ahead my friend and trust the process. Allow the Holy Spirit to heal you, cleanse you, and make you whole. When you become whole you are able to see differently.

Your worship time increases, your testimony of what the Lord has brought you through is able to speak volumes to other people as Christ has redeemed you. So, go ahead and walk out the process and then be sure to help someone along the way.

You dear one have an amazing story to tell. You don't respond the same, you are concerned with how you are bearing fruit and winning souls for the kingdom of God. You know that you have developed a strong prayer life. You look different.

Most importantly, you have a better understanding of the peaks and the valley experiences of life and you can now posture yourself in prayer and speak to that situation, that mountain, that barrier, that obstacle, and tell it be thou moved now in Jesus name Amen! Whew!!!!!!! Give God Glory!

Be Free

DAY THREE

Isaiah 61:1-3 (NLT)

Good News for the Oppressed

The Spirit of the Sovereign Lord is upon me, for the Lord has anointed me to bring good news to the poor. He has sent me to comfort the brokenhearted and to proclaim that captives will be released and prisoners will be freed. He has sent me to tell those who mourn that the time of the Lord's favor has come, and with it, the day of God's anger against their enemies. To all who mourn in Israel, he will give a crown of beauty for ashes, a joyous blessing instead of mourning, festive praise instead of despair. In their righteousness, they will be like great oaks that the Lord has planted for his own glory.

Listen friends, I just want to begin to give God all of the glory, honor, and praise because the Lord is with me wherever I go. There is no place that I can go that He is not with me. I am so thankful that God is my shelter, my comforter, my peace, my strength when I am weak, He is my coach when I need to be encouraged and He is my joy when the pain of this world hits me and tries to enter my mind, my thoughts and silence my voice from what man thinks and has rejected me.

I am shouting and dancing with joy with my hands lifted high in the sky because the Lord has anointed me which causes me to be protected from the enemy and all of his traps and schemes that he tries to ever so slickly and cleverly trick me trying to trip me and make me fall and stumble into the old man, the old lifestyle, But I rejoice because of the new "me" The new inner man who dwells inside of me.

Because of God's grace and mercy which follow me 365 days of my life I am able to use my voice strong, loud, powerful and without fear or being anxious to tell everyone I know, everyone I meet, everyone that comes in contact with me about God's great compassion that he has towards me and you.

That's good news for all of us, God cares about the poor man, God cares about the rich man, God cares about the sinner man, God cares about the back slider, God truly cares about our broken hearts, God cares about our failures, God cares about our shortcomings, God sees you. Yes you!, and He wants to let you know that you are valuable, you are smart, you are needed, and you are creative!

There are unique ideas hidden in you that the world needs to see. You are not invisible. Now, rise from that low place and see yourself in the way that God our Heavenly Father views you.

You have been released from anything that tries to have you bound down to struggles, worries, and burdens and depression. You have been freed in Jesus name.

Isn't that some good news!!!!!!!!!! BE FREE!!!!!!!!!!!!!!!!!!

Spirit Lead Me When I Call

DAY FOUR

Psalm 32:8 (NLT)

The Lord says, "I will guide you along the best pathway for your life. I will advise you and watch over you."

My dear friends,

May the Spirit of the True and the Living God guide you in all of your decisions that you have to make regarding all areas of of your life that include:

Your job, finances, children, health concerns, your family, your mind, will, and emotions, your mood and how you feel.

May the Spirit of the True and the Living God always answer you by fire. May you understand with clarity the way that you should go. The answer that you should respond with either giving a Yes or No not at this time. May you fully begin to sense spiritually the leading and guiding and prompting of the Holy Spirit as angels are being released to assist you get to where you need to be.

May you always be sensitive to know when the Lord is instructing you that if you continue making the same choices that you are making right now that you will end up with the same results. Beloved, you should be further along than where you are at.

Listen, you have been given another chance. Go and get in your quiet place wherever it is that is quiet and peaceful for you. Put your cell phone, tablet, smart watch, and any other distraction in a room separate from your quiet place.

Now, just grab a notepad and a pen. Grab some Kleenex-tissue and just begin to open your mouth and cry out to Holy God. Tell him how much you love him, tell him how much you need him, tell him how much you depend on him, Tell him how you surrender everything to him.

Tell Abba Father how you can't make it without him and that you need to hear from him. You are lifting up holy hands unto the Lord and asking for his instructions, his wisdom, his safety plan for your life, his loving arms of protection holding you, his hand guiding and pointing you in the right direction on the right path.

The God we serve and love wants nothing but the very best for you in this life. He wants you to walk with power and authority, He wants you to speak with words of victory coming out of your mouth and not the language of defeat, doubt, and regret.

Are you ready to fully let go of the unnecessary stress that comes from "doing it my way" Why don't you try "Yes Lord! Yes to your will and to your way, for your word declares to me that you will guide me along the best pathway for my life!" Thank you Lord, I Trust You. Thank you Lord, I choose you today!

Keep Making Those Daily Confessions!

DAY FIVE

Philippians 4:13 (NKJV)
I can do all things through [a] Christ who strengthens me.

Welcome back friends,

I am so pleased that you are here to continue on this journey together. I am so excited to share some good news with you. Guess what, you can make it! Yes you. Please don't let the storms of life that you may be facing right now overwhelm and burden you.

One of the things that I want to start having you to really exercise daily in your life is making the confession that I can do all things through Christ who strengthens me. Listen friends, I want to remind you that if you are a born-again believer you have the Holy Spirit living inside of you.

And guess what, He really wants to help you. He wants to see you reach your goals, have a successful life, and have peace in your heart, mind, and soul. I don't want to leave anyone out or left behind, so I always want to address anyone who does not know Jesus Christ as their personal Savior.

You can make a decision right here right now to let Jesus enter into your heart by saying this prayer. Now, the next steps that you would want to take is making sure that you get connected to a local church in your community that you can have the opportunity to learn, grow, and become a part of a wonderful supportive community of other believers.

Romans 10:9 New King James Version That if you confess with your mouth the Lord Jesus and believe in your heart that God has raised Him from the dead, you will be saved.

So, friends I just want to share that you can begin again. Learn to change your thinking and develop more positive thoughts and small goals to allow yourself to celebrate your successes. So, buckle down and dedicate yourself to set times to begin focusing on goals. Take your time and allow yourself to succeed at the goals you set for yourself.

Go Back and Do It Again

DAY SIX

Scripture Reference: 2nd Corinthians 1: 3-11 (NLT) We will focus on verses 3-6.

In this passage of scripture, we find that Apostle Paul is writing a letter to the Church of Corinth. Apostle Paul is giving an encouraging word to strengthen, equip and continue to build up the faith of the people.

So, I would like to do the same and speak a word of life to you today. I wanted to let you know that no matter what you may be facing today that is challenging you, stressing you, or coming against you that you should be encouraged and strengthened in your faith to know that *"God Offers Comfort to All"!* Hallelujah!!!!

In this particular passage of scripture, we learn through God's word that God gives us some specific details....and we must pay attention to them. God reveals to us that He is:

Verse 3. Our merciful Father and the source of all comfort.
Merciful-compassionate, forgiving, and tenderhearted towards his people.

Source-The beginning.

Comfort-You have freedom from any pain or physical distress. "You can simply "rest" with no worries."

Verse 4. God comforts us in all of our troubles so that we can comfort others!

Verse 5. So even when we *"suffer" which means go through something bad or unpleasant* we can still help others……

Verse 6. Even when you begin to examine, look at, review your situation. You will be comforted.

So Here are Some Things That We Can Do:

1. Learn to develop and have patience.
2. Learn to endure-remain and stay in the process that you are going through until it has been fully completed.
3. Be confident and rest in the Lord that he will see you through whatever you may be facing today.

And last but not least my friends. You must develop an Action Plan!

I'd like to share some scriptures with you so that you may be able to develop your own action plan.

Here are some Spiritual Tools for your Toolbox:

Matthew 6:33 (KJV) "Seek the Lord" But seek ye first the kingdom of God, and his righteousness; and all these things shall be added unto you.

Psalm 32:8 (NKJV) "Ask the Lord for Directions"

I will instruct you and teach you in the way you should go; I will guide you with My eye.

Habakkuk 2:2 (KJV) "Write out the Vision"

And the Lord answered me, and said, Write the vision, and make it plain upon tables, that he may run that readeth it.

1st Corinthians 16:13 (NIV) "Stand Strong in your Faith"
Be on your guard; stand firm in the faith; be courageous; be strong.

Psalms 1 (KJV) "Have Wise Counsel"
Blessed is the man that walketh not in the counsel of the ungodly, nor standeth in the way of sinners, nor sitteth in the seat of the scornful.

Psalms 27:14 (KJV) " Wait Patiently on the Lord"
Wait on the Lord: be of good courage, and he shall strengthen thine heart: wait, I say, on the Lord.

Philippians 4:4 (KJV) "Rejoice in the Lord Always"
Rejoice in the Lord always: and again I say, Rejoice.

Now, I speak a word in due season unto your life and I charge each and everyone of you to ***"Go back and Do It Again"!***

Blessings!

Remember The Lord Your God

DAY SEVEN

Hello friends,

I want to share a brief prophetic word of exhortation with you.

Scripture Reference:

In Deuteronomy 8:18 (NKJV)

The word of the Lord declares…….

"And you shall remember the Lord your God, for *it is* He who gives you power to get wealth, that He may [a]establish His covenant which He swore to your fathers, as *it is* this day.

Friends, we are charged with a great responsibility on our part. We must:

1. Remember- which is having a mindset to be mindful and always keep God on your mind.

Friends, I just want to share with you that God will give you ideas, inventions that have not been thought of yet by man, he will cause you to write a book, novel, develop a play, create a curriculum, develop a policy/procedure that will benefit many lives everywhere.

God will provide you with musical scores to compose, produce and conduct. God will create new songs in your heart to record and perform for nations to hear, God will give you one single word or idea, thought to change your life, your destiny, your future, and God will launch you into your appointed destiny.

God will supply you with all of the tools you need, God will answer your questions that need to be answered for your specific assignment, God will set you up with everything you need in order to get you to the place you need to be to obtain the power to get the wealth.

God will cause doors to be open that no man can shut. God will give you favor with man when you thought it was over, when you had just made the statement, who's going to help me? And when God does meet you friend, at your appointed time with your appointed destiny.

You must never forget to:

Remember the Lord your God.
Remember where you come from.
Remember to keep yourself humble.
Remember to be connected to your Church/Spiritual Covering.
Always find a way to sow into the life of another person in need of help.
And finally, my friends, Always remember Jesus! Always keep him by your side and in your heart and take the Lord God with you "everywhere" you go.

Blessings!

Are You Following The Instructions That the Lord Has Given To You?

DAY EIGHT

Hello Friends,

Today I want to share some thoughts with you regarding following instructions. When we receive detailed instructions, we are being told exactly how something should be done. If we fail to follow instructions what happens? You said it.... Things don't work and go according to the plans.

Well friends, If you've been like me you have not always followed the instructions that you were given. That leads to unnecessary work, being tired, frustrated when you didn't have to be like that in the first place and so forth....

So, let's all Thank God that we can all look back and see when we have taken a shortcut in following instructions and now let's shift our focus on three examples from a biblical perspective and let's all receive a very powerful word on the importance of following instructions.

Scripture References:
Proverbs 8:33, Proverbs 16:20, and Joshua 1:7

Proverbs 8:33 (NIV)
Listen to my instruction and be wise; o not disregard it.

Proverbs 16:20 (NIV)
Whoever gives heed to instruction prospers, and blessed is the one who trusts in the Lord.

Joshua 1:7 (NIV)
"Be strong and very courageous. Be careful to obey all the law my servant Moses gave you; do not turn from it to the right or to the left, that you may be successful wherever you go.

Our first person that we will briefly look at will be Abram:

In Genesis Chapters 12, 13, and 15 we will take a look at how Abram through great courage and faith followed the instructions from God.

Genesis Ch. 12
(Promises to Abram)
So, we see that Abram left his country.

Genesis Ch. 13
Abram now inherits Canaan.

Genesis Ch. 15
God makes a covenant with Abram.
I would like to encourage you to continue reading your bible to see just how important it is to follow the instructions that God gives to you, God's power, grace, and mercy can change the destiny of your life!

Let's briefly look at another biblical example.

Noah:

Genesis 6: 8-22

Noah obeys God's specific instructions and builds the ark. And then the great flood came.

And our final example that we will look at will be Joshua.

Joshua:

Joshua Chapter 6: 3-6

You shall march around the city, all *you* men of war; you shall go all around the city once. This you shall do six days. And seven priests shall bear seven trumpets of rams' horns before the ark. But the seventh day you shall march around the city seven times, and the priests shall blow the trumpets. It shall come to pass, when they make a long *blast* with the ram's horn, *and* when you hear the sound of the trumpet, that all the people shall shout with a great shout; then the wall of the city will fall down flat. And the people shall go up every man straight before him."

Hallelujah!, The walls of Jericho came tumbling down!

Friends, may I ask what instructions have you ignored from God? What instructions have you not followed from God? What has God specifically to you do? What has he told you to let go of and you want to hold onto it? After all of these examples my prayer is that you will

Follow the Instructions that the Lord Has Given to You.

Blessings!

What Are You Waiting On?

DAY NINE

Hello Friends,

I want to say Thank you to everyone who has been a part of reading these daily devotionals. I pray that your soul is being refreshed, restored, and renewed by the word of the Lord. I pray that you are finding new inspiration and I pray that you are being challenged to grow and increase your level of faith.

This devotional focuses your attention to begin to examine and look at and ask yourself the following question. "What ***Am I Waiting On?"***

Scripture Reference: Psalm 32:8 (NKJV) I will instruct you and teach you in the way you should go; I will guide you with My eye.

Friends, I have some questions for you. I want you to listen and then think about your honest answers for just a few moments okay....

Have you ever received instructions from the Lord? Okay, Have you followed those instructions that were given to you? Did you move, flow, operate in the direction in which The Holy Spirit told you to?

Have you followed the path that God has led you on for that business idea? Clothing line?, Nail shop?, Barber and Beauty Shop?, That Catering Business?, That Counseling Service?, That Photography Studio?, That Janitorial Business you want to open?

Have you received a confirming word that Yes, you you are headed in the right direction? Have you been given a Word of Wisdom regarding how to develop and implement your plan so that you can be blessed for your obedience and begin to see the Mighty hand of God move on your behalf? Watch supernatural doors open for you as you begin to move and operate in your destiny and your plan and purpose for your life.

But still you have not moved on God has spoken to you? Can I speak a word in due season to you my friend and tell you that God will take care of you?

Not only do we have the reassuring word from the main scripture Psalms 32:8 but we also have Jeremiah 29:11 (NIV) For I know the plans I have for you," declares the LORD, "plans to prosper you and not to harm you, plans to give you hope and a future.

Now friends, I just want to encourage, strengthen, and equip you to continue to move forward with what God has planned for you. Continue to spend time with God, hear God's voice and seek God's face.

Give God Glory and watch how according to His word (Psalm 32:8) **8** I will instruct you and teach you in the way you should go; I will guide you with My eye.

Again, I ask you friends............ ***"What Are You Waiting On?*** "

Blessings!

The Lord is My Shepherd

DAY TEN

Scripture Reference: The 23rd Psalms

Hello Friends,

With this devotional I wanted to share some inspirational and uplifting thoughts when you look at "The 23rd Psalms" we will look at several ways the psalmist communicates to us and lets us know just how personal and intimate this is in our relationship with God.

Psalms 23 (KJV) The Lord is my shepherd; I shall not want. He maketh me to lie down in green pastures: he leadeth me beside the still waters. He restoreth my soul: he leadeth me in the paths of righteousness for his name's sake. Yea, though I walk through the valley of the shadow of death, I will fear no evil: for thou art with me; thy rod and thy staff they comfort me. Thou preparest a table before me in the presence of mine enemies: thou anointest my head with oil; my cup runneth over. Surely goodness and mercy shall follow me all the days of my life: and I will dwell in the house of the Lord forever.

Verse 1. In the Amplified Version of the Bible, it illustrates that the Shepherd "to feed, to guide and to shield me" And the New Living Translation Bible ends the sentence by stating that "I have all that I need." (This tells me and reassures me that "provision and protection" are made daily for me)

Verse 2. In the Amplified Version of the Bible, it is illustrating that The Lord lets me lie down in green pastures; and The Lord leads me beside the still *and* quiet waters. The New Living Translation points out that The Lord leads me by peaceful streams.

So, Verse 2, Let's me be comforted in knowing that I may lay down in safety, peace of mind, peace in my body and have peace in my soul……. Hallelujah! I can have tranquility! It also lets me know it is a place of stillness, quietness, "no worries in God, no anxiety, depression, agitation, concerns, fears, doubts, struggles, obstacles, barriers, hardships, In God.

Why…….???????

Because Verse 3 tells us…. In the Amplified Version of the Bible that God, "refreshes *and* restores my soul (life);

The New Living Translation encourages us even more by saying, "He renews my strength. He guides me along right paths, bringing honor to his name."

So, we have a clear picture that God our Father, Our Shepherd continually shows His love to us by:

Refreshing us…..

Restoring us…….

Renews us………

Strengthens us……..

Guides us……….

All along the RIGHT PATHS……….

Verse 4. Even when I have my darkest days in front of me and I am not able to see the light, even when I feel "weighed down"-vexed, stressed, hindered, unfocused, unable to see clearly, hear clearly, think clearly. Because I am troubled and worried on every side. The word of God declares that "I don't have to fear any evil for you are with me. The Amplified Version says that God's rod is always there to protect me! And the staff is always there to guide me and together they provide healing to me mind, body, and soul by providing comfort and strength, reassurance to me.

The New Living points out that you are "Always Close Beside Me"!

Verse 5. The Amplified Version reminds us that we are always being "Refreshed when we read the word of God, Renewed when we read the word of God and Energized when we read the word of God."

The New Living Translation says it like this, You honor me by anointing my head with oil. My cup overflows with blessings.

That you recognize me, respect, and honor me by anointing my head with oil,,,,,,,,, and I am spilling out and running over with God's favor and protection, provision, grace, and mercy! Oh!!!!!!! Hallelujah, Praise God!!!!!!!!!!

Verse 6. The Amplified Version points out God's unfailing love for each and every one of us on a daily basis. And that All of the days of my life, I will dwell (live) in God's presence. The New Living says it like this, That God's goodness and unfailing love will pursue me all the days of my life,

Which means God's never-ending love will always chase me, pursue me, cover me, and protect me Forever more 24 hours a day, seven days a week.

It is my prayer that this has been a Blessing unto you!

It Had to Happen This Way

Day Eleven

Hi Friends,

Today, I would like to give you some words of encouragement. I'd like to challenge and stretch your faith in a new direction, and I would like to encourage you to be Believe God and Trust Him and to continue to remain strong in your "Wilderness Experience."

Your time where you are alone with God and He is again, stretching your faith, increasing your faith and total dependence on Him alone, For you see my friends, It is not in your job, your family, your money, your possessions, your friends or in that relationship/object that you may be holding onto so dearly, But it is ALL in Christ Jesus from whom our blessings flow and we have our being (Acts 17:11)

Remember, your wilderness experience is a part of your process and development for your life. *"It had to happen this way"!*

Scripture Reference: Jeremiah 29:11, James 1:2-8 and Psalms 27:14

Friends, you can rejoice because no matter what you may be facing God has a plan and a purpose for your life. (Jeremiah 29:11) God wants to see you walk on the path of righteousness for his name's sake. (Psalm 23:3) God wants to see you eat the good of the land.

** If you are first willing and obedient. (Isaiah 1:19) So, we see that we are required to do some things in order to reap the benefits (blessings) "harvest" from the Lord. When we look at James 1:2-8 the word of God encourages us to....

My brethren, count it all joy when you fall into various trials, knowing that the testing of your faith produces patience. But let patience have *its* perfect work, that you may be perfect and complete, lacking nothing. If any of you lacks wisdom, let him ask of God, who gives to all liberally and without reproach, and it will be given to him. But let him ask in faith, with no doubting, for he who doubts is like a wave of the sea driven and tossed by the wind. For let not that man suppose that he will receive anything from the Lord; *he is* a double-minded man, unstable in all his ways.

And finally, I would like to end this with Psalms 27:14. After you have done all that you know to do. You must just simply stand, rest, remain quiet and wait patiently on the Lord to give you some clear instructions, For the word of the Lord declares in Psalms 27:14

Wait on the Lord: be of good courage, and he shall strengthen thine heart: wait, I say, on the Lord.

Remember, It had to go this way. For God to get the Glory, For you have grown closer to Him, You have can go and be a witness to someone else and tell them that they can make it.

You can share your experiences as God has been a Healer, Deliverer, Savior, Doctor, Lawyer, Master Teacher, Provider, He's been your Shelter, He's been a Way Maker, He's been and always will be your All and All.

Blessings!

Pray, Press, Push, Now Release

Day Twelve
Scripture Reference: Philippians 3: 13-14

Hello Friends,

I wanted to originally do this devotional with the scripture reference of (Philippians 3: 13-14). This devotional is entitled....

"Pray, Press, Push, Now Release!"

But the Holy Spirit has completely changed this message. And has instructed me to share the following message with you on this particular day.

The message that you are about to hear is a direct Rhema word from the Holy Spirit to me as I wrote it in my *"Book of Remembrance."* And so, I share and release this word with you as I am commanded to do so.

I speak to each and every one of you that will hear the sound of my voice in this podcast and I tell you that it does not matter what situation you may face today you must *"Pray without ceasing, Press toward every goal that you have given to accomplish, Push every obstacle, distraction, out of your life and leave it alone, Let it go, Never to return to it.... And now Release everything over to Almighty God,*

Your Mind, Your Will, Your Emotions, Everything!!!! God wants You! All of You!!!!! Now when you make a choice to truly surrender and submit unto Holy God let Him lead, guide, teach, and complete a work through you and in you as you walk it out by faith in your own personal journey. Your Wilderness Experience."

Question: Will you say YES.........

Book Of Remembrance Entry:

Thursday July 12, 2018

I just wanted to start by thanking The Holy Spirit for everything! That has happened, that will happen, and that shall happen in my life! In Jesus Mighty Name Amen!

Last night, as I was going to sleep after saying my prayers and also very early this morning at 5:00am The Holy Spirit had taken me in the realm of the Spirit, and I could see very clearly through the dream I was having, and this is what the Holy Spirit said unto me both on last night and this morning:

That I am about to be launched off "TO THE NATIONS"

"Just like a rocket is being launched by NASA into outer space. The launch pad site has been secured with only the people who have security access granted by me (The Holy Spirit) to be in direct contact with you."

"You, Daughter, are in the stages that are FINAL and are ready to be launched for the entire world/universe and Nations to receive you."

"Everything is almost complete; you are receiving the final instructions as I have given them to you to make this launch date that is targeted a success on the first try with no malfunctions."

"Because Daughter, you have been obedient, you have been a servant and continue to be a servant, you are faithful, you are trustworthy, you are a friend, even when people didn't treat you right and they hurt you and disappointed you, you still did the right thing though it was very hard, difficult, and painful at times."

"You maintained your character and your representation of who you are by being a representative of me! Because That fits who you are! My Daughter!"

"I've taught you many, many, many lessons in your wilderness experience where I personally trained, equipped, prepared and now I AM launching you OFF to "Complete and Fulfill" your Destiny and your Assignment to the Body of Christ…"

"To the lost who walk in darkness, to the hopeless, the helpless, the sick and the diseased, to the emotionally fragile, the wounded, to all the captives that need to be set free and need to begin to walk in the marvelous light!"

"To those who need to be restored and reconciled back unto me, to the backslider, to the liar, to the cheater, to the doubter, to the alcoholic, to the drug addict, to the woman chaser, to the man chaser, to the perverted mindset, to the twisted thoughts, to the spiritually wicked…"

"To the carnal man, to the bound soul, to the unjust, to the corrupt, to the unclean spirit, and to the ungodly to save their souls have them accept Jesus in their heart and confess Him with their mouth to receive Jesus Christ as their Personal Lord and Savior."

"I now send you My Daughter and release you to the "NATIONS" for every man to harden not their hearts but the very day that they hear my voice through your words the people will come running saying what must I do to be saved. Saved for real, no playing this time. I want to surrender and submit it ALL to Jesus!"

"For you, My Daughter are to be My Apostle, You are to be "All things to All Men" that's how "The Nations" will see you. (I've already told you this and broke all of that down in your book of remembrance). According to my word in 1st Corinthians 9:19-23"

"Now, I have been commissioned, ordained, anointed, appointed, and prepared you for such a time as this. Go and preach the Gospel of Christ EVERYWHERE and Go in my name! For you have been commissioned and authorized by my hand and my authority."

Matthew 28: 19-20
Acts 1:8
Acts 19:11
For I have spoken, says the Lord of Host!

You Must Make A Choice: Choose This Day Whom You Will Serve

Day Thirteen
Scripture Reference: 1st John 3: 6-11 (AMP)

Hello Friends,

I'm here today to speak a very powerful word to you. I am charged to tell you to choose this day whom you are going to serve.... You must make a choice. Are you going to serve God or are you going to serve Baal?

You must come out from them and be separate, Says the Lord. Touch no unclean thing, and I will receive, welcome you. (2 Corinthians 6:17).

Jesus wants to see you live a healthy, complete whole, full, balanced life and walk in victory over the hand of the enemy. But you must make a decision.... You cannot hold onto the world "Egypt" and do the things of the world and then wonder why you don't walk in victory in your life. When you make a willing and active choice to stay in a sinful lifestyle God cannot bless you. You have made a choice to live separate from Him.

So today my friends, I pray that you hear my voice, make a choice, let it go!!!!!! Let him go!!!!!! Let her go!!!!!!!! Return to Jesus! He loves you! Friend. There's no valley too low that He cannot stop and reach His arm out to catch you!

Can I prophesy and tell you today my friend that God sees you, God hears you, God loves you, God understands you, and most of all God cares for you!!!!! Be not dismayed - distressed, upset, agitated, fearful, worried, or concerned....

God will take care of you, but you have to do your part and you must make a decision and do your part..... Won't you return back unto Him.....Come unto Jesus while you still have time. Love you and God Bless Each and Every One of You!!!!!

The Blood Still Works

Day Fourteen
Scripture Reference: 1st John 1:9 (AMP)

Hello Friends,

I'm so excited about this prophetic exhortative word! It is good news... Amen. Great news!!! We all have sinned and fallen short of the glory of God. We all have made mistakes. We have not been perfect all of our life.

But the word of God declares that if we ADMIT that we have sinned and CONFESS our sins, HE is faithful-dedicated, committed, consistent and loyal HALLELUJAH! And just and will FORGIVE us of OUR SINS and Cleanse us CONTINUALLY! From all unrighteousness- our wrongdoing, everything that is not in conformity (lines up) with His will and purpose.

Hey, Hallelujah I simply declare unto you that "THE BLOOD STILL WORKS"!!!!!!!! And It will never, ever lose its Power!

Blessings!

Access Granted

Day Fifteen
Scripture Reference: Ephesians 2:18 (NLT)

Hello My Dear Friends,

We have not only the Good News, which is the Gospel of Jesus Christ, We have access, direct access to go boldly before the throne of grace and pray and talk boldly to the Lord and Savior Jesus Christ for ourselves. Hallelujah! So, go for it!

Be bold, take your plans, your thoughts, your ideas, your concerns, your questions, your burdens and take it to the Lord and let Him give you wise counsel, Let Him lead, guide, direct, and order your steps.

God wants to see you succeed friends. God wants to see you blessed, God wants to see you walk in a lifestyle of victory where you are shining bright for all men to see and they are now telling you… I see that you look different, I want what you have…

How did you get that? What is that? Go ahead, Be a witness for Jesus! Tell others about the love, grace, mercy, favor, goodness, favor, promotion, advancement, made a way out of no way for you…

Tell Him how God has kept you….. Go ahead, get excited, tell everybody how God protected you and kept you safe, Go ahead, tell everybody how God paid that outstanding bill that only He could do.

Go ahead and tell somebody how you were able to keep your home, your job, your car, your child's needs have been met, there was a positive in the bank account instead of a negative.

Go ahead and tell somebody that as you walk upright before the Lord that the Lord is blessing and keeping you…Once again, Access is granted!

Power Thoughts Reflections Of Psalm 103

Day Sixteen

Welcome Back Dear Friends,

Psalm 103 New Living Translation (NLT)

Psalms 103 emphasizes praise unto the Lord. Notice that in this particular Psalm there are no requests being made to the Lord. It is only praise being given. This is the fourth book (division) of the Numbers of Psalms, which contain Psalms 90-106 which all deal with "Praising God".

V. 1-6 Deals with Personal Praise to the Lord.

V. 6-18 Deals with National Praise to the Lord.

V. 19-22 Deals with Universal Praise to the Lord.

A Psalm of David.

Let all that I am praise the Lord; with my whole heart, I will praise his holy name. (True praise comes from a grateful heart. "All that is within me means my inner focus is on the Lord. my heart, my soul, my mind and my strength"). Let all that I am praise the Lord, may I never forget the good things he does for me. He forgives all my sins and heals all my diseases. He redeems me from death and crowns me with love and tender mercies. He fills my life with good things.

(I want to point out that in versus 3-5 David listed six special blessings from the Lord. They are 1. Forgiveness, 2. Healing, 3. Redemption, 4. Love, 5. Satisfaction and 6. Renewal.)

My youth is renewed like the eagle's! The Lord gives righteousness and justice to all who are treated unfairly. He revealed his character to Moses and his deeds to the people of Israel.

(This verse refers to God leading the Children of Israel by the Glory Cloud, His word, and His Prophet). The Children of Israel knew God's acts, but Moses knew God's ways. (Why he was doing it).

The Lord is compassionate and merciful, slow to get angry and filled with unfailing love. He will not constantly accuse us, nor remain angry forever. He does not punish us for all our sins; he does not deal harshly with us, as we deserve. For his unfailing love toward those who fear him is as great as the height of the heavens above the earth. He has removed our sins as far from us as the east is from the west.

(In verses 8-12 we have a summary of what Moses learned about God on Mt. Saini. Ex. 33:12-13, Ex. 34: 5-9, and Numbers 14:18) The pictures of v.8-12 are that of a courtroom. In which God is both Judge and Prosecuting Attorney. He has all of the evidence he needs to condemn us, but he does not prolong the trial. *** When the judge is your Father, and when Jesus has gone to trial and already died for our sins there is full and free forgiveness to all who ask for it.

The Lord is like a father to his children, tender and compassionate to those who fear him. For he knows how weak we are; He remembers we are only dust. Our days on earth are like grass; like wildflowers, we bloom and die. The wind blows, and we are gone— as though we had never been here. But the love of the Lord remains forever with those who fear him. His salvation extends to the children's children of those who are faithful to his covenant, of those who obey his commandments!

2 Corinthians 6:14-18 New Living Translation (NLT) *** References v. 17-18 but the reading begins at v. 14

Don't team up with those who are unbelievers. How can righteousness be a partner with wickedness? How can light live with darkness? What harmony can there be between Christ and the devil? How can a believer be a partner with an unbeliever? And what union can there be between God's temple and idols? For we are the temple of the living God. As God said: "I will live in them and walk among them. I will be their God, and they will be my people. Therefore, come out from among unbelievers, and separate yourselves from them, says the Lord. Don't touch their filthy things, and I will welcome you. And I will be your Father, and you will be my sons and daughters, says the Lord Almighty."

2 Corinthians 7:1 New Living Translation (NLT)

Because we have these promises, dear friends, let us cleanse ourselves from everything that can defile our body or spirit. And let us work toward complete holiness because we fear God.

*** This Psalm also points out that we should not forget the blessings of God after we receive them and enjoy them.

The Lord has made the heavens his throne; from there he rules over everything. Praise the Lord, you angels, you mighty ones who carry out his plans, listening for each of his commands. Yes, praise the Lord, you armies of angels who serve him and do his will! Praise the Lord, everything he has created, everything in all his kingdom. Let all that I praise the Lord.

(In v. 19-22 When we worship the Lord, we are worshiping the King! We are worshiping the Lord of Host. who is sovereign over all things. As, I come to a final close, Let's remember what David did in 1st Samuel 17:45

1 Samuel 17:45 New King James Version (NKJV)

Then David said to the Philistine, "You come to me with a sword, with a spear, and with a javelin. But I come to you in the name of the Lord of hosts, the God of the armies of Israel, whom you have defied.

So, as we close out this teaching of Psalms 103. Let us join corporately together and think about the goodness of God, Think about all that He has done for you, Think about His tender mercies, and His loving kindness, Think about how He has been your all and all and let's corporately do v.1.

Psalm 103:1 King James Version (KJV)

Bless the Lord, O my soul: and all that is within me, bless his holy name.

Power Thoughts: I Don't Talk I Just Listen

Day Seventeen
Scripture: Main Foundation Scripture Proverbs 3: 5-7

Proverbs 3:5-8 New Living Translation (NLT)

Trust in the Lord with all your heart; do not depend on your own understanding. Seek his will in all you do, and he will show you which path to take. Don't be impressed with your own wisdom. Instead, fear the Lord and turn away from evil.

Proverbs 3:5-7 Amplified Bible (AMP)

Trust in *and* rely confidently on the Lord with all your heart and do not rely on your own insight *or* understanding. In all your ways know *and* acknowledge *and* recognize Him, and He will make your paths straight *and* smooth [removing obstacles that block your way]. Do not be wise in your own eyes; Fear the Lord [with reverent awe and obedience] and turn [entirely] away from evil.

Proverbs 3: 5-8 Msg. Bible:

Trust God from the bottom of your heart; don't try to figure out everything on your own. Listen for God's voice in everything you do, everywhere you go; he's the one who will keep you on track. Don't assume that you know it all. Run to God! Run from evil!

The Lord will work out the plans for my life!!!!!

Psalm 138:8 Amplified Bible (AMP)

The Lord will accomplish that which concerns me; Your [unwavering] lovingkindness, O Lord, endures forever—Do not abandon the works of Your own hands.

VERY IMPORTANT:

Proverbs 3:8

It will be health to your body [your marrow, your nerves, your sinews, your muscles—all your inner parts] and refreshment (physical well-being) to your bones.

*** A sinew is your tendon. It connects and ties muscle to the bone tissue.

Ezekiel 37:4-14 (AMP)

Again He said to me, "Prophesy to these bones and say to them, 'O dry bones, hear the word of the Lord. Thus says the Lord God to these bones, 'Behold, I will make breath enter you so that you may come to life. I will put sinews on you, make flesh grow back on you, cover you with skin, and I will put breath in you so that you may come alive; and you will know that I am the Lord. So I prophesied as I was commanded; and as I prophesied, there was a [thundering] noise, and behold, a rattling; and the bones came together, bone to its bone. And I looked, and behold, there were sinews on the bones, and flesh grew and skin covered them; but there was no breath in them. Then He said to me, "Prophesy to the breath, son of man, and say to the breath, 'Thus says the Lord God, "Come from the four winds, O breath, and breathe on these slain, that they may live. So I prophesied as He commanded me, and the breath came into them, and they came to life and stood up on their feet, an exceedingly great army.

The 23rd Psalms

Day Eighteen
Psalm 23

Blessings and Greetings to each of you Dear Friends as you read this devotional. May God richly bless you.....

At the center of the bible is the book of Psalms. This great collection of songs and prayers expresses the heart and soul of humanity. In them we find the whole range of human experiences expressed.

David and other writers honestly poured out their true feelings reflecting a very dynamic and powerful life changing friendship with God. Throughout the Psalms the writers do the following:

Confess their sins
Express their doubts and fears
Ask God for help in times of trouble
And finally Praise and Worship The Lord

As you read the book of Psalms,

1. you will **hear** believers crying out to God from the depths of despair,
2. you will **hear** them singing to him in the heights of celebration.

3. ***You will always hear them sharing honest feelings with their God.***

People often turn to the book of Psalms for comfort during times of emotional struggle, unnecessary stress and when they are facing pain. It is in this time that we are able to discover the power of God's everlasting love and forgiveness.

The Authors of Psalms

David wrote 73 Psalms

Asaph wrote 12 Psalms -He was one of David's musicians. He was one of the worship leaders in the Tabernacle. (1st Chronicles 6:31-32).

He was also known as a Prophet.

The sons of Korah wrote 9 Psalms - They were singers in the choir and they also were bakers for meat offerings. (2nd Chronicles 20:19).

Solomon wrote 2 Psalms

Heman with the sons of Korah wrote 1 Psalm

Ethan one of the four sons of Mahol wrote 1 Psalm

Moses wrote 1 Psalm

There are 51 Psalms that are anonymous.

The 23rd Psalms

Verse #1

David wrote the 23rd Psalms out of his own experience of spending his early years with caring for sheep. (That's why he describes the Lord as a Shepherd). *Reference: 1st Samuel 16: 10-11.*

Sheep are completely dependent on the shepherd for provision, guidance, and protection.

The New Testament identifies Jesus as the Good Shepherd. (John 10:11)

Hebrews 13: 20 identifies Jesus as the Great Shepherd.

1st Peter 5:4 identifies Jesus as The Chief Shepherd.

And we the sheep are obedient followers who are wise enough to follow the good shepherd who will lead us in the right places and lead us the right way we should go.

The qualities that we have as sheep are evident by our discipleship… "Being followers of Christ"

1. We are passionately committed to follow Jesus
2. We are sensitive and submissive to the Holy Spirit.
3. We study the word of God and apply it to our everyday life.
4. We are not distracted by the world's standards and recognize and walk as "Children of the Light and not as Children of Darkness."
5. We recognize and understand that our body is the temple of God. We are to walk in holiness with our thoughts, deeds, as an act of genuine worship.
6. Finally, we understand that we are created to have a personal relationship with Jesus Christ our Lord and Savior. We are to talk with Him, spend time with Him, Worship Him, Pray to Him and spend some time waiting on Him to speak to us and share the good news with others by being a witness to someone who does not know who Jesus is.

Verse #2

When we allow God our Shepherd to guide us that is when we have contentment. Our Shepherd knows the *"green pastures"* and the *"still waters"* that restore each and every one of us. ** *We can only reach that place by following The Shepherd and by being obedient to Him.*

**When we choose to sin and go our own way we cannot blame God for the environment that we have created for ourselves. When we rebel against the Good Shepherd we rebel against our own best interest.

When God leads us on the path of righteousness ***He*** instructs us through the word of God.

The ***"still waters"*** are pleasant, peaceful, which flow from the fountain of the rivers of the "***living water***" which shall never run dry. It flows from Immanuel's veins!!!!!

He restores my soul- When the storms, trials, issues of life cause me to hurt and pain "***He***" restores me, refreshes me, and replenishes me. The Lord our God is the one who heals thee…. Exodus 15:26 says He sends His word to heal our disease. He is the Lord our Healer…. SO, what is it that you need healing from?

A diseased mind?
A diseased mouth?
A diseased heart?

Our God restores us when we stray away from Him and become "***lost***" when we HELP God Out by……Taking a different path rather than staying on the one He told you to because it's taking too long and I'm not seeing any results fast enough… God lovingly shows us our error and we confess our sins and repent and He receives us once again with His arms always open. The Lord is our strong tower… He will continue to lead us, guide us, direct us, and increase our faith.

Here are the Seven Levels of Faith

1. Weak Faith-Romans 4:19 Faith that limits God
2. Temporary Faith-Luke 8:13 Faith that believes for a while but when the test starts to come it fails.
3. Active Faith-James 2:14-26 Faith that masters all enemies it pumps it up and your faith becomes active.
4. Strong Faith- Romans 4:20 Faith that refuses defeat.
5. Great Faith- Matthew 8:10 & 15:28- Faith says, Whatever is spoken it shall be done. This is the kind of faith that moves God.
6. Unfamed Faith- 1st Timothy 1:5 & 2nd Timothy 1:5- Faith that does not boast or brag or put on a show.

7. Perfect Faith- Galatians 2:20 Absolute faith. Standing on God's word.

Verse #4

God is always with us. He will never leave us nor forsake us. Even when we face danger, when we WALK through the valley of the shadows of death, THERE is no evil in it IT is only a shadow…. DEATH cannot separate believers from the Love of God. It can do us no harm… God's presence is with us and the gospel is called the rod of Christ which comforts us under the protection of Almighty God. Psalms 110:2

Verse #5

God provides all things for us… Our physical, social, emotional, spiritual, social, financial wellbeing. We as believers have 24-hour access. YOU must access it by using the right key……..

Question

Does your key fit correctly?

Are you able to have access granted to what you're needing?

Has your access been delayed but not denied because you're still going through the process and you're not quite ready to receive what He has planned for you yet?

God offers protection to His sheep when enemies surround us ** Psalm 91- A Psalm of Protection, Blessing and Covering.

The table that is set and prepared for us is one of abundance. This cup is filled with Provision…. There is always enough. You never have to worry about running out or running short… YOU are always covered!!!!

Verse #6

Goodness and Mercy follow the believer all the days of our lives……

WE have:

Pardoning Mercy

Protecting Mercy

Sustaining Mercy
Everlasting Mercy

As I come to a close. I'm reminded of part of one of my Dad's sermons where he talked about The Lord calling a meeting and He called:

Love
Joy
Peace
Patience
Kindness
Faithfulness
Gentleness
Self-Control

But when The Lord called for Goodness and Mercy they can never answer roll calls on time. They always show up late and their dirty, smelly and their robes are torn. So, Mercy gave an answer of why they always arrive late and have to leave at a moment's notice. ** Because when the sheep go astray and are wandering around in darkness outside of the light We hear a humble cry saying Lord, Have mercy on me…. And we have to go running to see them. Goodness shields them from the Evil One and gets them out of the "***STANDING WATER***" where there is danger, SEE you cannot see the Evil One in the Standing water, It lurks below the surface, You fall in and you're now in the dirt, filth, trouble, sin, and you need HELP… That's when Mercy comes in to see you and COVERS you when you should have been exposed, cleaned you up, and led you back to the right place where you are supposed to be….

That's why VERSE 6 says Surely Goodness and Mercy shall follow me ALL the days of my life!!!!!! And I shall DWELL in the house of the Lord FOREVER, FOREVER, FOREVER AMEN!

Provision

PROVISION (This is a direct download given to me journal entry)

Day Nineteen
Philippians 4:19

Blessings unto you!

I was just sitting here on my bed and I was watching a Lifetime Christmas movie and I reached and grabbed my cellphone to look at the days remaining in this year. As I was looking at the calendar I noticed that on next Friday it will be December 18th.

That day may not mean much of anything to you, but it is very significant to me. You see December 18, 2019 was the last day that I worked at a full-time job. The Lord called me into full time ministry. Now, with all of that being said that gives the title of this devotional. "Provision."

Let me tell you that God will provide for you. Provision is your portion for every area of your life just like I am a living witness of God's provision for my life. But, let me say this and be very clear about this....

You must understand that <u>you must be in righteousness for this to happen</u>. I have to live a life completely yielded and surrendered to God. Once again, I tell you that the Lord will take care of you. You will not lack just as Psalms 23 is written. The Lord will take care of your food, shelter, clothing, your health, safety, and protection. The Lord cares for you. Don't worry the Lord will provide!

The Whole Armor of God

You Must Stay Dressed *"Don't Take Off Your Wardrobe"*

Day Twenty
Ephesians 6:11-18 (NKJV)

Hey Family Welcome Back!

In this devotional you will learn the importance of making sure why you must remain completely dressed in your spiritual armor on a daily basis.

It is very important for every believer to not only stay dressed but definitely have an understanding as to why it is necessary to remain dressed and engaged for any spiritual battle or spiritual warfare or attack that may come your way.

Every believer must always be on guard, watch and pray and be aware and alert of the enemy so that when at a moment's notice you have been placed under an attack and have a strike come against you, you will already be equipped, armed and dangerous, loaded ready to not only battle and fight but to win and gain victory over each and every area of your life.

Now, let's look at the scripture and gain a better understanding of what it means to put on the whole Armor of God. In this devotional.

I will also utilize other supporting scriptures in the bible to continue to help you build your faith up and further equip you with the necessary tools to fight this spiritual warfare. Amen! Let's go and look at these scriptures.

Pieces of Armor and What They Are Used For:

Belt- Girded around your waist. "The Truth"
Breastplate- "Righteousness"
Footgear- "Spreading the Gospel" The Good News
Shield- "Faith"
Helmet- "Salvation"
Sword- "Word of God"

Verse 10

Finally, my brethren, be strong in the Lord and in the power of His might.

The first thing that I would like to do is breakdown three very important keywords that are being used in this sentence. 1. Strong 2. Power 3. Might Let's take a deeper look and gain a better understanding of what Apostle Paul is teaching.

We are being encouraged, strengthened, refocused, and instructed as to what we are to do… be strong. So, if we are to be strong we must first make sure that we have a clear understanding of what that means… (as defined by the dictionary) It means to be able to withstand great force or pressure.

"That will come against you" …………Q: How many of you have had great forces or pressure come against you? Have you been strong when this happened? Again, not strong in your strength but in the strength of the Lord? We'll talk more about this as we go through the webinar.

We must next look at the word power and gain a better understanding of the *"Power of God"* when we talk about the power, we are also again referring back to God's strength as well. We are to know and understand that God El-Shaddai, God Almighty. Is on our side. He is Sovereign "over everything!"

Now, let's look at the last word might. Might is a great power of strength.

So, we already have a very clear understanding from verse ten alone that no matter what anyone of us may face in our life we have " El-Shaddai" God Almighty who has All Power, All, Authority, All, Dominion, On your side and God alone is able to withstand any force or pressure that will ever come against you!!!!!!! You should be rejoicing and giving God Glory right there!!!!!

Verse 11

Put on the whole armor of God, that you may be able to stand against the wiles of the devil.

Here once again in verse eleven we are given instructions to follow….. We are to put on the whole armor of God so that means to always have it placed on our body (in our heart, mind, will and emotions). To leave it on at all times so that we will always be in a position and be prepared ready to engage in any spiritual battle that may come your way…..

You will be prepared again fully armed, locked, and loaded to return fire with (The word of God) from your sword in any direction that the attack may come, whether it is from the North, The South, The East, or the West. You will be able to stand strong in the power of God's might as we have just learned and been reminded of. Hallelujah!!!!

And the second part of that verse continues to say that you may be able to stand against the wiles of the devil.

You will be able to maintain your position, you will not be changed in your thinking, point of view or in your attitude in what God has for you.

So therefore, the tricks, schemes, games, and lies of the devil will not sway you. Because you are now aware and using your discernment and will not allow yourself to get caught up or entangled in mess. I want to remind you once again of the subject of this webinar. *The Full Armor of God* - You must Stay Dressed *" "Don't Take Off Your Wardrobe"*!!!!!!!!!

Verse 12

For we do not wrestle against flesh and blood, but against principalities, against powers, against the rulers of the darkness of this age, against spiritual *hosts* of wickedness in the heavenly *places.*

So, we must now look at some key words in this verse. The Apostle Paul is making it very clear that we are not wrestling against flesh and blood……. So, let's first get a very clear understanding of what he means when he says "wrestling"

We are not engaging in combat (physical, mental, or emotional) *you're not going to get inside my head and try to change/challenge my thoughts,* {1st Corinthians 2:16 (KJV) For who hath known the mind of the Lord, that he may instruct him? But we have the mind of Christ}.

So therefore, I also know that I am not going to allow myself to get into struggles, have difficulties, or take blows towards another person via hand-to-hand combat (fist to fist action) or by the use of my tongue where I begin to speak and say things in a verbal exchange with you.

Because The word of the Lord declares in 1 Timothy 2:8 New Living Translation (NLT)

In every place of worship, I want men to pray with holy hands lifted up to God, free from anger and controversy.

Let's continue to study the word of God and apply it to our life by now looking at other word principalities. When the word "principalities" is broken down, it becomes defined as: divisions, fields, lands, regions, or nations for an example.

Now, let's look at the word rulers, it is also defined as: The crowned head not to exclude some of the following examples, kings, queens, monarchs, a lord, or a prince (Legalistic).

The word darkness is defined as: wickedness or evil, the total absence of light.

The word spiritual host is defined as: The prince of the air and all of its wickedness.

It is, the continual opposition against anything that is Holy unto God which would include: Walking the in the light, which is God's truth, But the enemy would like to promote anything connected to the following: pride, malice, fraud, and unbelief to name a few of its characteristic traits.

Remember, The devil wants to use any method he can to get you to turn away from God and enter back into a life of sin and iniquity.

So, you must do the following according to the word of God
1 Timothy 6:12 Amplified Bible (AMP)
Fight the good fight of the faith [in the conflict with evil]; take hold of the eternal life to which you were called, and [for which] you made the good confession [of faith] in the presence of many witnesses}.

You must engage in battle as we discussed in the beginning of this webinar with your spiritual armor. So, use them! Use your sword, which is the word of God, and use your words to declare his praise! Let this scripture in

Psalm 51:15 King James Version (KJV)
O Lord open thou my lips; and my mouth shall shew forth thy praise}. Be

another tool in your spiritual toolbox of weapons to fight against the enemy.

Verse 13

Therefore take up the whole armor of God, that you may be able to withstand in the evil day, and having done all, to stand.

There are two things that I would like to mention here. *The first thing that you must do is make sure that you take up the whole armor.....* Your armor that you are wearing is very important, it is priceless, it must not ever be forgotten, slacked upon, become damaged, mistreated, unattended, forgotten or abandoned, or simply thrown away....

My God, by this I make reference to where you completely turn and walk away from God and become a child of darkness, returning fully back to Egypt.

The carnal world and the pleasures there of... This is a very dangerous place to be in when you are absent from the presence of God and have become out of the ark of safety.

The word of God makes it very plain to us in several versions of the bible of how important it is to as the title of this webinar tells us to remain in *The Whole Armor of God*-You Must Stay Dressed *" "Don't Take Off Your Wardrobe"*

The Word of God Declares That in The ....

NIV says.....Therefore put on the full armor of God
NKJV says.... Therefore, take up the whole armor of God
NLT says......Put on every piece of God's armor
AMP says.... Put on the complete armor of God

Now, the next thing that you must be able to do is stand,

You must maintain your position, you cannot waver, you cannot fall, you can't get tired, worried, worn out, your thinking must be clear, you must have a plan, you must remain focused, you cannot become weak, wounded, or give up, YOU MUST

STAND!!!!!

So, my friends, you must continue to use your full, complete, whole armor for this fight that you are in... I want to again encourage and strengthen you in the Lord with another tool for spiritual toolbox.

The word of the Lord declares in

2 Chronicles 20:17 (NIV)

You will not have to fight this battle. Take up your positions; stand firm and see the deliverance the Lord will give you, Judah, and Jerusalem. Do not be afraid; do not be discouraged. Go out to face them tomorrow, and the Lord will be with you.

I just want to remind each and every one of you that God is with you!!!!!!! Hallelujah!

Verse 14

Stand therefore, having girded your waist with truth, having put on the breastplate of righteousness,

You must know the truth which is God's Holy Word. God's word securely and tightly fastens every area of our being so that we will always walk in the truth, talk with the truth and not be a person of wrong motives or wrong intentions, shady, sneaky, looking solely out for yourself and what you may stand to profit or gain. You must defeat Satan, who is the accuser of the brethren,

You must also remember what {Proverbs 4:23 (KJV) tells us. Keep thy heart with all diligence; for out of it are the issues of life}.

Our heart is another major area that often comes under attack from the enemy. We as believers are to always keep our emotions in check. You manage them, but you may ask what do I mean by them? (How you think, how you feel, how you respond, how you talk) Don't let your emotions manage you..... Okay, Let's take this to the word of God once again and make sure our armor is on correctly. We will look at two scriptures.

1. *{Galatians 5:22-23 (AMP) But the fruit of the Spirit [the result of His presence within us] is love [unselfish concern for others], joy, [inner] peace, patience [not the ability to wait, but how we act while waiting], kindness, goodness, faithfulness, gentleness, self-control. Against such things there is no law}.*
2. *{1st Peter 5:8-9 (AMP) Be sober [well balanced and self-disciplined], be alert and cautious at all times. That enemy of yours, the devil, prowls around like a roaring lion [fiercely hungry], seeking someone to devour. But resist him, be firm in your faith [against his attack—rooted, established, immovable], knowing that the same experiences of suffering are being experienced by your brothers and sisters throughout the world. [You do not suffer alone.]*

Verse 15

and having shod your feet with the preparation of the gospel of peace;

We should always be prepared to share the Good News with everyone that we encounter, We should always have a word of encouragement to share with someone who is in need, we should be able to pray with or for someone when it's needed, we should be able to give a praise report or a testimony to share with someone and tell of God's goodness and how He made a way out of no way for you,

We should be able to give a scripture to someone who needs to look at and be able to hold onto it and study it. And finally, we should have some signs and indications in our own personal lives that we have power and that we walk with victory and that we shout with a voice of triumph to the Lord our God.

Verse 16

above all, taking the shield of faith with which you will be able to quench all the fiery darts of the wicked one.

This is where you must keep your faith going strong.....you must recognize the enemy for who he truly is. You must know that the enemy will use anyone or anything to get you out of your peace in God, the enemy will attempt to shift your focus and your mindset that you have,

Let's look at some identifiers/signals that you are being baited for a trap and then let's follow that up with the word of God by once again applying biblical scriptures to support "The Armor "of which we should always have on daily for our protection.

Indications that you are being baited......when signs of the following things begin to happen....

You are getting offended easily.....

You are getting in your feelings and feel that you are being slandered by others....

You can't fully let go and deal with "old wounds/past hurts" that you should have received healing from by now but no, you choose to remain dwelling in the past, and make statements like this...They did this...So, I am filling...It continues with he did, she did, etc...The cycle won't ever end because it has not been dealt with at the root of the issue). We'll discuss that in another webinar.

Other things to be aware of are "setbacks."

This is when you begin to have repeat occurrences with roadblocks, obstacles, hurdles difficulties and complications appear to come from everywhere and on every side on a constant basis. Question: Does any of this sound familiar to you? Have you been in this situation?

As I mentioned earlier, Let's turn to the word of God and see what the scripture has to say and how we should respond to further support "The Full Armor of God - You Must Stay Dressed *" "Don't Take Off Your Wardrobe."*

John 14:27 Amplified Bible (AMP)

Peace I leave with you; My [perfect] peace I give to you; not as the world gives do I give to you. Do not let your heart be troubled, nor let it be afraid. [Let My perfect peace calm you in every circumstance and give you courage and strength for every challenge.]

Verse 17

And take the helmet of salvation, and the sword of the Spirit, which is the word of God;

I want to encourage you my friends, to begin to think strategically if you have not already been doing so. It is very important that you know the following two scriptures and apply them to your life so when the enemy tries to come to you and wants to have you do the following things....

Start doubting everything
Begin to operate in fear
Start wondering Who You Really Are...
Question yourself, Did I really hear this from the Lord..
Am I really doing the right thing?
Is this the will of God for my life?

Then if you can relate to anyone of these statements let's immediately back all of this up with our sword which is once again the word of God and let's see what the scripture tells us.

John 10:27-28 Amplified Bible (AMP)

The sheep that are My own hear My voice and listen to Me; I know them, and they follow Me. And I give them eternal life, and they will never, ever [by any means] perish; and no one will ever snatch them out of My hand.

Philippians 4:8 Amplified Bible (AMP)

Finally, believers, whatever is true, whatever is honorable *and* worthy of respect, whatever is right *and* confirmed by God's word, whatever is pure *and* wholesome, whatever is lovely *and* brings peace, whatever is admirable *and* of good repute; if there is any excellence, if there is anything worthy of praise, think *continually* on these things [center your mind on them, and implant them in your heart].

Verse 18

praying always with all prayer and supplication in the Spirit, being watchful to this end with all perseverance and supplication for all the saints.

My dear friends, as we prepare to end this webinar with the last verse. Let's do exactly as it says, Let's pray humbly, let's pray in the Spirit, and let's always remember what the word of God says to do....

1 Peter 5:8-9 (AMP) Be sober [well balanced and self-disciplined], be alert and cautious at all times. That enemy of yours, the devil, prowls around like a roaring lion [fiercely hungry], seeking someone to devour.

*My final closing words and thoughts for this webinar e-course are the same as when I began this course. I want to speak directly into the life of everyone who views this webinar and tell you this...Don't ever take off, forget about, or think that you do not need..."The Whole Armor of God-*You Must Stay Dressed *"Don't Take Off Your Wardrobe"*

Your Affliction and Your Deliverance That Follows

(Your Process and Your Development)

Day Twenty-One
Psalm 34:17-20
English Standard Version

When the righteous cry for help, the Lord hears and delivers them out of all their troubles.
The Lord is near to the brokenhearted and saves the crushed in spirit. Many are the afflictions of the righteous, but the Lord delivers him out of them all. He keeps all his bones;

Welcome Back Dear Friends,

I just wanted to share another real raw relevant transparent moment with you. I pray that every time you read this daily devotional book that it ministers and speaks life to you, your mind, your body, your emotional wellbeing, your financial wellbeing, and your physical environment...

The very place where you feel that you are all by yourself. You really feel that no one else can possibly understand or relate to how and what you are feeling……. Or be able to understand, identify or comprehend how you may be feeling….

So, you continue to deal with the pain, you continue to deal and function in numbness and survival mode instead of having peace in your life……. I pray right now in this daily devotion for you my dear brother and my dear sister that in the name of Jesus it reaches you in that valley experience.

I pray that it reaches you when you feel as if you're stressed, pressed, or maybe you feel as if your back is up against the wall. I just wanted to take some time and have a conversation with you and let you know that the affliction you may be experiencing right now won't last forever.

Okay, let's talk about that because someone may be wondering what an affliction is…. An affliction is something that causes pain or suffering. It could also be a disorder "condition" that you have.

Which could be considered to look like anyone of these following statements: The affliction could be a disease, a complaint, an ailment, an illness, some type of suffering, discomfort and distress, pain, trouble, misery, hardship and or misfortune.

But that's not all….. It could include some of these feelings you may be experiencing any type of adversity, sorrow, torment, tribulation, cross to bear, (You may feel that the weight of the world is on your shoulders)

Or you may feel as if you have a thorn in your flesh/side. And last but not least you could feel as if I am experiencing another trial! Another ordeal! Well, remember what the title of this devotional book is. "God, I Thank you For Building Character In Me"…..

For I have good news to share with you…. That when the righteous cries out the Lord hears them and delivers them out of all of their troubles.....

So, If you are reading this and you do not know Jesus Christ as the Lord and Savior of your life I want to extend an invitation to you to accept Jesus as your personal Savior. Will you let him into your life today? If your answer is Yes, then simply repeat this prayer friends...

Romans 10:9-13 (New King James Version)

that if you confess with your mouth the Lord Jesus and believe in your heart that God has raised Him from the dead, you will be saved. For with the heart one believes unto righteousness, and with the mouth confession is made unto salvation. For the Scripture says, "Whoever believes on Him will not be put to shame." For there is no distinction between Jew and Greek, for the same Lord over all is rich to all who call upon Him. For "whoever calls on the name of the Lord shall be saved."

Now, You will need to be connected to a local body of Christ church home where you can continue to grow in the faith, mature and develop into being fully equipped in the body of Christ.

God Bless You!!! You just made the best choice in your life. I am rejoicing with you and for you. Now be developed and processed and finish strong on this faith walk!

I Know The Power And Authority That I Walk In

(I Just Send The Word)

Day Twenty-Two
Psalm 107:20 (NLT)

He sent out his word and healed them snatching them from the door of death.

Psalm 107:20 (AMP, CE)
He sends forth His word and heals them and rescues them from the pit *and* destruction.

Welcome back friends!

I just wanted to let you know that I don't be present there with you to pray for you. I am going to release a word of faith prayer to you and in this devotional I ask that whatever affliction, disease, infirmity, sickness that you have you will receive your healing by faith that you have been made whole.

I am sharing another teaching from my personal book of remembrance that I have been studying and received this download from the Holy Spirit. May it bless you right where you are at. May your pain be healed. May you continue to be water of the word in your life daily through reading your bible, praying, fasting, and worshipping the Lord and Savior Jesus Christ.

Sickness: The unhealthy condition of the body or mind.

Allergies
Colds and Flu
Conjunctivitis
Diarrhea
Headaches
Mononucleosis
Stomach Aches

This also includes any and all:

Ailments
Diseases
Disorders
Illnesses
Infirmities
Nauseous
Syndromes

Disease: An Abnormal condition they are medical conditions that are associated with symptoms and signs of the following:

Illness
Sickness
Infections
Disorders
Complaints
Conditions
Disabilities

Cancer
Virus
Defects
Abnormalities

Affliction: Something that causes hurt/pain.

Anguish- Severe mental or physical pain or suffering.

Calamity-An event that causes great damage, distress, or disaster.

Depression-Persistent loss in interest of activities. (It impacts daily living).

Difficulty-Struggling, stress, problems, pain, hassles.

Distress-Severe anxiety, constant worrying.

Grief-Deep sorrow, heartache, agony, sadness, mourning, misery.

Hardship-Adversity, misfortune, trouble, pain, trials, disaster

Misery-Great distress in the mind and body, torment, despair, and gloom.

Misfortune-repeated bad luck, setbacks, failures, tragedy, devastating blows that are continuous.

Pain-Physical suffering and discomfort.

Plague-Causes continuous trouble and distress.

Sickness-Unhealthy condition of the body and mind.

Sorrow-Deep distress caused by loss, misfortune, or disappointment.

Suffering-The undergoing of pain.

Torment-Severe mental or physical suffering.

Trial-Test, a formal examination that you go through.

Tribulation-Trouble, worry, anxiety, burdens, tragedies, traumas, setbacks, suffering, pain, or anguish.

Trouble-Difficulties or problems.

Woe-Great sorrows, distress, misery, pain, heartbreak, hardships, disaster, misfortune, unhappiness, suffering, or torment.

You may experience a warmth come through your body. You may experience chills as you read this. You may experience an immediate release and sense of joy and gratification. Keep praising the Lord! Keep rejoicing and thanking God for your healing. Keep speaking the word of God over your life daily.

God Bless You! Receive your healing by faith!

I Am Not In The Same Place This Year

...As I Was Last Year...Where Are You At?
Day Twenty-Three

Philippians 3:13-14 New Living Translation
No, dear brothers and sisters, I have not achieved it,[a] but I focus on this one thing: Forgetting the past and looking forward to what lies ahead, I press on to reach the end of the race and receive the heavenly prize for which God, through Christ Jesus, is calling us.

Welcome back dear friends!

I just wanted to stop and take a few minutes to see where you are at in your personal journey and your very own process? Are you still wandering around in the very same place that you were this time last year?

May I ask you what has been your motivation or lack thereof? In Philippians we find Apostle Paul teaching that he has not achieved it yet but one thing that he does is focus...

SO, who or what has your attention? May I just give you a word of encouragement and tell you don't give up and don't stop. WAKE UP!!!!!

Get your head back in the game. Focus on the short-term goals, focus on the long-term goals, focus on what you have been praying about, fasting for, and you have had dreams about at night. Stay focused…..

Don't give up now go and finish the book, write the business plan, create the clothing line, start your podcast, open your food truck, get a location, and set up a pop-up shop.

Just get it done. Go ahead, I believe you. You can do it…..And remember Apostle Paul's words… forget the past and look forward to what lies ahead.

Be All Things To All Men

Day Twenty-Four

1 Corinthians 9:19-23 (New Living Translation)
Even though I am a free man with no master, I have become a slave to all people to bring many to Christ. When I was with the Jews, I lived like a Jew to bring the Jews to Christ. When I was with those who follow the Jewish law, I too lived under that law. Even though I am not subject to the law, I did this so I could bring to Christ those who are under the law. When I am with the Gentiles who do not follow the Jewish law, I too live apart from that law so I can bring them to Christ. But I do not ignore the law of God; I obey the law of Christ. When I am with those who are weak, I share their weakness, for I want to bring the weak to Christ. Yes, I try to find common ground with everyone, doing everything I can to save some. I do everything to spread the Good News and share in its blessings.

Welcome Back Dear Friends,

I am so glad that we have almost made it to the end of the journey for this book. By now you have been challenged in your thought process, you have had to get in a quiet place and complete some self-examination to really challenge yourself to look and see what is truly important.

You have looked at what you focus and major on and also what you minor on... One lesson that I want you to walk away with is truly being all things to all men. I want to encourage, stretch, challenge you to move outside of your comfort zone.

I also want you to look at the people who are in your surrounding circle? Who are they? Why are they there? What is their role in your life? Do some people view and see you as a mother or father figure? A big auntie or uncle? A cool cousin, what role do you play in the life of the people surrounding you.

Well.....Apostle Paul teaches us an excellent lesson that we are to try to find a common ground with the people that are in our lives. I want to inspire each and every one who reads this devotional entry to be the sounding voice of stability, concern, wisdom, truth, honesty, integrity, moral and compassion to all of those dear treasured people in your life who call you friend.

I inspire you to live a life that challenges them to obtain and pursue a closer relationship with God, achieve higher levels of educational success, complete entrepreneurship endeavors, and pursue positive healthy whole relationships. Let them see Christ in you.

And last but certainly not least be authentically you flaws and all.... People need to see that you are not perfect no one is but you strive daily to live a righteous life and have a close relationship with God, and you live in peace with yourself and men.

Go Ahead Take A Deep Breath And Breath!

Day Twenty-Five

1 Peter 5:7 (Amplified Bible, Classic Edition)
Casting the whole of your care [all your anxieties, all your worries, all your concerns, once and for all] on Him, for He cares for you affectionately and cares about you watchfully.

Welcome back dear friends,

Let me start this devotional by asking you several questions okay? What's on your mind? What's troubling you? What's the big concern or mountain or obstacle that you absolutely wholeheartedly believe in your mind that you cannot "get around, bypass or plow through?"

Can I tell you okay as you are reading this that God sees you, God hears you, God understands you, God loves you, God knows all about what you are thinking, feeling, and going through. Guess what, God cares for you! God loves you! God wants you to do one simple thing.

Do you know what it is? Well, let me tell you. God wants you to talk and spend time with Him and tell Him everything that concerns your life, your job, your finances, your home. God really does want to hear what is making you feel stressed out, tired, frustrated, angry, upset, irritated, and agitated.

Because our devotional scripture addresses it all……. I get it! Life can sometimes deal you an unexpected storm that comes into your life, but I want to help you and equip you in how to deal with the storms of life.

Listen everyone that is reading this book can relate to being several of the occupations listed below all day every day so let's take the pressure off and use this devotional scripture and learn to just talk honestly to Jesus and cast all of our cares and give Him everything.

DO YOU WEAR THESE HATS ON A DAILY BASIS MULTIPLE TIMES DAILY???

"YOU ARE NOT PERFECT"

You are a chef preparing meals (Breakfast, Lunch, Dinner and Snacks oh! And all of those extra meals that you hadn't planned on cooking, but you made it come together for your family and whatever the situation was.)

A nurse giving 24-hour care to comfort and care

A therapist/counselor to help solve problems

Police to keep the family safe

Lawyer to stand up in your defense (your family)

Beautician

Accountant

Judge (keep the peace of family, friends, work, all)

Uber/Lyft Driver (constantly)

Performing Arts Specialist (you have learned to be creative at the drop of a dime to make or create anything at any time for any situation that could happen)

I just want you to always remember that the God we serve has the ability to heal me, keep me safe, love me, forgive me, stand for me on my behalf, protect me, love me unconditionally despite all of my faults and shortcomings...

Let the process and development in your life begin to teach you, mold you, shape you into who it is that you are called and purpose to be. Now, surrender and submit yourself to the process, learn and grow!

Listen, I can't wait to hear your testimonies friends. I look forward to reading them as you complete this devotional book. Please send your testimonies in please see the contact information at the end of this book.

Blessings! Love You All!

I Know I've Got To Do Something Different!

Day Twenty-Six

Romans 8:37 New King James Version
Yet in all these things we are more than conquerors through Him who loved us.

Listen Friends!

Do you feel as if you are being stretched? Do you feel as if you keep doing the same thing and getting the same results? Well, let's consider that now you need to look at doing something different.

Can I ask you if you have ever stopped to take the time and ask The Holy Spirit what is it that you would like for me to do today? What are your plans for my life? Because what I'm doing is not going anywhere.

Do you ever feel that you are missing something, and you just can't put your finger on what it is? Well friend, It's simple, you have said yourself....

You have been trying to do everything yourself. But can I tell you that God wants to lead you, guide you, and help you in your everyday life.

So, I just wanted to encourage you that in every situation you face that feels impossible, every mountain that stands in front of you you can speak to it.

Begin to speak to all of the storms that pop up in your life as a crisis situation that you were not expecting at all. I just want to tell you again, friend that you are more than a conqueror.

And that you will make it through your valley experience. You will come out of the storm you are in and you will get to the other side! Now, Praise God! I am rejoicing with you.... Because you are more than a conqueror!

You Must Always Be Prepared

(This is a direct download given to me journal entry)

Day Twenty-Seven

Acts 1:8 King James Version
But ye shall receive power, after that the Holy Ghost is come upon you: and ye shall be witnesses unto me both in Jerusalem, and in all Judaea, and in Samaria, and unto the uttermost part of the earth.

Hey friends,

Welcome back! I am so glad you are continuing to learn and grow on this journey with me as you are investing in yourself by really taking a deep look at what's important in my life right now, what I value in my life, and most importantly how I am choosing to spend my time and energy.

So, are having lots of energy drains or do you feel as if you have made it to a better place in life on this journey. One of the things that I would like to share with you is always being prepared to share the gospel.

Yes, that's right "The Good News" with everyone you meet. Listen, there is someone out there who needs to hear your voice, your testimony your story about how you have experienced some "#situations" in your life. They need to hear that Girl yes you can make it or Dude, Bruh, Man.... Let me tell you, we are going to make it and you will be alright. "I got you" .....

Okay, I had to break this down so that you can see that everybody is reachable and teachable. Does that make sense? Remember that people just want to hear YOU.... They just want the truth.....for example you might pass by a homeless person, buy them a meal if you don't want to give them any money.

Who knows, that might have been a part of your story and someone gave you a chance. Another thing to remember is that with the homeless population everyone does not have the same story and you would be surprised to know that some of the homeless population is made up of former business owners, military personnel, etc....

Remember as our scripture tells us.........

That we are to be witnesses in Jerusalem, and in all Judaea, and in Samaria, and unto the uttermost part of the earth.

Here's what your Jerusalem looks like.....Jerusalem would be you sharing "the good news" with your family, friends, neighbors, co-workers and also the people in your city where you live.

Judea looks like.....The people that live in the same state that you do.

Samaria looks like......The United States of America the USA.

The utter most parts of the earth...... Would be the global continents, international and globally. Not to exclude the Third world countries as well.

So, you see my friends, there are so many opportunities for you to share the good news with someone. You can pay it forward with buying someone's purchase behind you. Be a witness, let your light shine brightly. The world needs your shining bright glow to bring someone some hope.

Many blessings unto you! Pay it forward!

You Have To Be Prepared To Work Hard To Get It!

Day Twenty-Eight

1 Peter 5:8 Amplified Bible, Classic Edition
Be well balanced (temperate, sober of mind), be vigilant and cautious at all times; for that enemy of yours, the devil, roams around like a lion roaring [in fierce hunger], seeking someone to seize upon and devour.

Welcome back dear friends,

I just wanted to start this devotional with having a discussion about putting the time in to do your work. There is one thing in this life that you have to realize. You must be present in the moment, you must be focused, you must be diligent and purposeful in what your goals are that you are trying to reach in your life.

Listen, you cannot be scattered and all over the place you must be well balanced. In this life, you can be absorbed and consumed with so many other things that can easily distract you. So, it is highly important that you are maintaining a daily schedule routine which would speak to being well balanced. This would also incorporate that you are taking care of your mind, your body, and your soul.

Another thing that I would like to point out is that you also have to make sure that your physical health is well balanced also. You must be mindful about how much grease intake and carbohydrates you take into your body. This can make you tired and sluggish.

Your mind begins to slow down, and you will want to take a nap instead of seizing the day and complete your goals and work the vision plan that you have set yourself…. Yes, I am reminding you to complete the vision, do not sleep and rest on the vision. You must also be cautious-be aware, careful, and yes even mindful of your environment.

Those who are in your environment and you must be aware of what they are speaking in your life and most importantly you have to be careful of what you are hearing… What you are receiving through your ear gates.

So, with that being said, I have a question for you. Who and what are you allowing to have close access into your life? I want you to stop and think about that for a moment and self-evaluate and see if this is a wise move or see if you need to move around…..Do not let anyone steal your joy or your peace.

Listen to me, Do not let anyone allow you to come out of your character. You must know who you are and where you are going. So, remember what I have said. Do not allow anyone to devour you…. In other words, don't let anyone destroy your character, ruin your name, devalue you, despise you, use you or bring any harm to you in any shape, form, or fashion.

Just a final tip for you. If the person in your life cannot value you, respect you, validate you in public, acknowledge you in public but only wants to see you in private (RUN FAST)…..

Then you might want to rethink: am I being watchful, sharp eyed like an eagle about anything that concerns my life and my wellbeing? Do they have my best interest at heart? Stay woke and remain focused. Do not lose focus of your goals that you have set for yourself. You know what they are. Now, go get that.

Bachelor's Degree
Master's Degree
Business Plan Written
Coffee Shop
Clothing Boutique
Real Estate License
Make Partner in the Law Firm
Establish Home Ownership

You can do all things through Christ who strengthens you! So just refocus, reset, and now continue to move forward. You've got this.

I'm proud of you.

Blessings!

Lord, I Need You To Lead Me And Guide Me

<u>There, I Said It. I Need Your Help. Help Me!</u>

Day Twenty-Nine

Psalm 32:8 Amplified Bible, Classic Edition
I [the Lord] will instruct you and teach you in the way you should go; I will counsel you with My eye upon you.

Welcome back friends,

I'm so glad that you are enjoying this devotional book. I look forward to reading your testimonies, your thoughts as you have made a choice to take a journey along with me as you learn and discover more of the word of God and grow in your relationship with Him.

I want to start this devotional with asking you some more questions. I feel by now that you are getting acquainted with my style of writing and learning my voice through written words.

Have you ever had to make bill arrangements? Have you ever had to reprioritize things? Have you ever had situation after situation happen to you in your life? Have you ever felt as if your family and friends questioned you or just didn't understand you? Maybe possibly even thought that things that happened to you were your fault?

Well, I just wanted to give you a word of encouragement. Please know that you are not alone. There are other people who have experienced this too. Can I ask you another question? Have you ever felt like you really weren't for sure which direction you were supposed to go?

Well, you are not alone. Are you trying to figure out what you should do with your career? Are you considering moving to another state or even out of the country? Do you need help with deciding what college to attend? Are you needing to have questions answered about whether this is the right relationship for me? Is this the right church for me? Should I get this new car?

Listen, life is full of every kind of question that you could have that pertains to everything. Yes, I said everything. It deals with your life, plans or thoughts you may have for your children, what moves to make in your career, what neighborhood you should purchase a home, But please let me take some of the pressure off of you if I may do so.

Have you ever thought about talking to God and asking Him first about what you should do? Go ahead, take a minute, and think about that...I'll wait. Now that you have taken a few moments to think about this and you have probably considered a list of people that you have talked to.

I want to ask you why have you not started with asking God? Listen friends, this devotional scripture really wants to point out that God is concerned about every area of your life. Yes, He really is concerned.

The Lord really wants to be a part of your life, your decision-making process only if you will allow him to.

Listen Jeremiah 29:11 Amplified Bible, Classic Edition

For I know the thoughts *and* plans that I have for you, says the Lord, thoughts *and* plans for welfare *and* peace and not for evil, to give you hope in your final outcome.

Wow! Isn't that great news? God cares so much about you that if you choose to accept him as your Lord and Savior He has plans to give you hope which is an expectation of a desired outcome for your life.

So, now that we have talked about that scripture about just how much he cares for you let's get back to God giving you guidance.

In Psalms 32:8 The Lord wants to teach and instruct you about how you should accomplish everything in your life. But the best part is that The Lord tells you upfront I will do this if with my eye upon you in the way that you should go. Here's the bottom-line friends.

You have to make a choice. You have to ask yourself do you want the leaching, leading, and guiding of the Lord or are you going to say, I know what I'm doing, I can do this on my own, can't nobody tell me what to do I don't need any help, I've got this.

Let me just tell you No, you don't, and you are going to end up in a worse place than where you started from. Listen you purchased this book so that you could study daily devotionals that will help you improve the quality of your life.

One of the very first things that you have to do is admit that I still need some help with my journey. I don't know it all and I am embracing my teachable moments as I realize that I am walking out being processed and developed in my character and it is for my good.

So therefore, I will admit that sometimes it's hard for me to admit what the title of this devotional says...That okay I need help. Help me. Beloved, I am proud of you! You are making more progress than you know. Now be blessed and enjoy your day!

Do You Have Some Jonah Tendencies In Your Life?

Day Thirty

The Book of Jonah Chapters 1-4

Hey friends welcome back! I just wanted to go through the book of Jonah with you and illustrate some life lessons. When you are reading this, I ask that you take the time and see where this is applicable in your life present day or past tense. I pray that this devotional meets you at your appointed place of need for growth, process, and development.

Jonah Chapter One

Do you find yourself running away from God when He tells you to do something?

Do you want to act as if you have all of a sudden become tired and can't do what He told you to do?

Do you get a flat-out attitude and refuse to do what God has told you to do?

Jonah admitted that he ran away from God's instructions, but he submitted to God and followed His instructions of what He told him to do in the first place.

Jonah Chapter Two

Jonah made the statement that "As my life was slipping away I remembered the Lord. (2:7)

We can oftentimes act like Jonah meaning-When life is going well we will take God for granted but when things start getting difficult, hard, unmanageable, or even unbearable then we will quickly cry out to the Lord to help us.

When we have a consistent daily relationship and fellowship with God we can seek him in both the good times and the bad times of our life. God really does want to be a part of our everyday life. Will you let him in?

Make sure that you do not let anything, or anyone take first place in your life. God is first and foremost in our daily lives.

Jonah Chapter Three

Even Though Jonah ran away from God's instructions that He had given to him Jonah was given another chance. Guess what you have that same opportunity just in case you did not do what you were supposed to do.

The Good News is for everyone who will receive it. When Jonah finally delivered the message in Nineveh like he was instructed the people received the word of the Lord and immediately repented from their wicked ways.

Are you sharing the good news with anyone that you come in contact with? You just might be the voice that the world is waiting to hear from.

Jonah Chapter Four

Jonah admitted the real reasons why he ran in the first place. Can you admit when you are wrong? And then do you go back to correct the damage that has been done?

Sometimes we secretly want to see people have some suffering for what they have done but the God we serve is a compassionate and loving God. And so, we should also be kind, patient, loving and we should want to help our sisters and brothers and give them a word of correction with love and understanding.

I Made It!

Day Thirty-One

Today you will have two scripture references for this very last devotional. I thought that these two scriptures would be very inspiring, uplifting and words of encouragement. Remember this scripture.

(Romans 10:17) King James Version
So then faith cometh by hearing and hearing by the word of God.

Romans 5:3-5 Amplified Bible, Classic Edition
Moreover [let us also be full of joy now!] Let us exult and triumph in our troubles and rejoice in our sufferings, knowing that pressure and affliction and hardship produce patient and unswerving endurance. And endurance (fortitude) develops maturity of [a]character (approved faith and [b]tried integrity). And character [of this sort] produces [the habit of] [c]joyful and confident hope of eternal salvation. Such hope never disappoints or deludes or shames us, for God's love has been poured out in our hearts through the Holy Spirit Who has been given to us.

2 Corinthians 4:8-9 Amplified Bible, Classic Edition
We are hedged in (pressed) on every side [troubled and oppressed in every

way], but not cramped or crushed; we suffer embarrassments and are perplexed and unable to find a way out, but not driven to despair; We are pursued (persecuted and hard driven), but not deserted [to stand alone]; we are struck down to the ground, but never struck out and destroyed;

Congratulations my dear friends!

You've made it to the end of this thirty-one-day devotional and the end of your journey with me in this series. Now, you will begin a new chapter in your life and prayerfully you take some of these life lesson devotionals along with you.

I thought that it would be fitting to end on such a high note of life lessons that over the years I've learned on my own personal journey my story of being processed and developed, refined, purged, consecrated for God's use, and equipped to advance the Kingdom of God.

I can't wait to hear your testimonies, your thoughts as you have taken this journey with me and along the way hopefully you have grown and you are not in the same place emotionally, physically, spiritually, psychologically, environmentally that you were in before you read this book.

May your life be forever changed with just a willingness to say Lord, I'm willing to be processed and developed by you. Develop my character, mold me, make me, and shape me into what you would desire me to be.

I'll do it. And for everyone on my journey that is in my story please be patient with me.... God is not through with me yet. *#beingprocessedanddeveloped.*

I may have had some setbacks, some delays, some unexpected disappointments, heartache, and pain in my life on my journey but I made it! I have learned to quiet my mind, body, and soul to be still and present before the Lord.

I have learned to listen and follow instructions and value the lesson being taught from the teacher. I have learned how to discipline myself. I have a much better skill set of how to manage my time effectively and wisely.

I have learned to value and implement wisdom in my life. I have dedicated a greater amount of time to what is truly a priority in my life. I have learned to say no and be okay with saying no, I'm not able to at this particular time.

I have grown in my own personal love languages so that I may pour out to others in a great volume and be impactful. I can honestly and truly say that I have learned to be okay with people not knowing the whole full story but only trusting what they heard from another person.

I have learned to smile when I may have wanted to cry… I have learned to remain strong in my faith and continue to confess the word of the Lord over my life, my family, my situation. I have learned that there is a blessing in being patient and waiting.

I also wanted to say that I hope you have also learned and are practicing doing two of the following things.

Don't see the world through damaged eyes. I pray that you will see with a new sight.

(2nd Kings 6:17) New Living Translation
Then Elisha prayed, "O LORD, open his eyes and let him see!" The LORD opened the young man's eyes, and when he looked up, he saw that the hillside around Elisha was filled with horses and chariots of fire.

Don't hear the world through damaged ears. I pray that you will hear with a new sound and revelation.

(Acts 17:11) New Living Translation

And the people of Berea were more open-minded than those in Thessalonica, and they listened eagerly to Paul's message. They searched the Scriptures day after day to see if Paul and Silas were teaching the truth.

Photo by: Excell LaFeyette, Jr.

About the Author

Prophetess Tina Mosely is a native of Tulsa, Oklahoma. She attends and serves faithfully in the ministry under the Apostolic covering of Apostle Towanda Stallings at the Okmulgee Community Church in Okmulgee, Oklahoma and also works in Apostolic leadership under Apostle Dennis Hardwell who is the Senior Pastor of Oasis The Place of Refreshing Ministries.

Prophetess Tina has birthed the launching of Tina Mosely Ministries and actively serves faithfully in the spreading of the gospel of Jesus Christ. It is a personal mission to see that everyone has the opportunity to accept Jesus Christ as their personal Lord and Savior.

Prophetess Tina is an active mentor role model in the community in which she lives. She is a member of Alpha Epsilon Omega Graduate Chapter of the Alpha Kappa Alpha Sorority Incorporated.

Prophetess Tina is a graduate from the University of Oklahoma, Masters Degree in Human Relations. Prophetess Tina is a Licensed International Chaplain Director.

Booking information for: Tina Mosely Ministries

P.O. Box 481052, Tulsa, OK 74148 (918)986-7799

prophetesstina@tinamoselyministries.org

Made in the USA
Middletown, DE
02 March 2023

25954377R00060